Random Writings

Random Writings: A compilation of poems, short narratives and random thoughts
Copyright © 2024 by Catherine Shelby Hale

Published in the United States of America

Library of Congress Control Number: 2024914692
ISBN Paperback: 979-8-89091-616-7
ISBN eBook: 979-8-89091-617-4

All rights reserved. No part of this publication may be reproduced, stored in a retrieval system or transmitted in any way by any means, electronic, mechanical, photocopy, recording or otherwise without the prior permission of the author except as provided by USA copyright law.

The opinions expressed by the author are not necessarily those of ReadersMagnet, LLC.

ReadersMagnet, LLC
10620 Treena Street, Suite 230 | San Diego, California, 92131 USA
1.619. 354. 2643 | www.readersmagnet.com

Book design copyright © 2024 by ReadersMagnet, LLC. All rights reserved.

Cover design by Ericka Obando
Interior design by Don De Guzman

Random Writings

A compilation of poems, short narratives and random thoughts

CATHERINE SHELBY HALE

Family Home Holidays

Grandma

Grandma, you waited for my birth with the joy of my mother
And from that moment on, you loved me like no other
You laughed when I laughed and wept when I wept
Through all of my life, loving vigil you kept
Grandma, to come to your house was such fun
To crawl in your bed when the day was done
I remember the feel of your hands washing mine
I never thought then I would see this time
Now you are the one who needs the care
Your days are lived in your bed and a chair
The circle of life is nearly complete
It won't be too long until the ends meet
Then I, you granddaughter, as no other
Will mourn your passing
With the grief of my mother

Someday

Someday-They'll come to you with thoughts that make you smile
They'll tell you all your efforts were worthwhile
They'll come to you and whisper, "Mom, we never knew
Just how much you loved us and what you tried to do"
Someday- His wife will tell you he picks up his clothes
And trims the lawn with care each time he mows
You'll smile thinking back when he thought life meant only fun
No matter what you threatened, his chores were never done
Someday-The home she makes will be straight as a pin
Love and sweetness will be found therein
You'll smile thinking back to that mess she called her room
At times her very presence filled the house with gloom
Yes, Someday-the glory of your life will be revealed
All the hurts and scares will long be healed
The Holy Ghost will whisper, Woman now you see
You are God's true partner, Mother eternally

Together

In our youth we discovered together
And soon we had fallen in love
We started out on a life of hope
Our marriage blessed from above
Together we created babies
Far finer than we'll ever be
We made a choice family together
Our children, you and me
Together we worked in our business
All day and late into the night
Together we faced our problems
Together our burdens seemed light
Together we shared joys and sorrows
Some hard times, some bad and some good
At times we thought we can't make it
But together we knew we would
The future is always uncertain
Except there will be you and me
Together is our promise
And the way we are meant to be

Adoption

I'm so glad that I'm adopted
So grateful that my birth mom opted
To let me have a life and live it with
The best mom and dad a kid could have
I'm so glad my birth mom chose
To see my life had fewer woes
By picking out for me
The best mom and dad a kid could have
She went through all the pictures
The stories and the files
She looked for loving people
To help me through life's trials
She prayed to Heavenly Father
To help her find the best
And you're the ones she chose for me
At the end of her long quest
I'm so glad that I'm adopted
I love you and I'm glad you opted
To share your life with me
You're the best mom and dad a kid could have
Added to your family tree
Yours throughout eternity
I will always try to be
The best kid a mom and dad could have

Ego Trip

I'm going on an ego trip
Don't know when I'll be back
I'm feeling hopeful self-esteem
Instead of just the lack
My husband is my sweetheart
My children are my friends
I'm seeing new beginnings
Instead of futile ends
I'm going on an ego trip
Unsure when I'll be back
I'm going to count my blessings
And put them in my pack
I haven't traveled down this road
For such a long long time
I'm laying down my heavy load
And oh it feels so fine
I'm going on and ego trip
Just starting on my way
The scenery looks so lovely
I think that I'll just stay

Sweet Sixteen

Sweet Sixteen, a well-known phrase
It's been used through the years
Less likely in these troubled times
With pressure from your peers
Sweet Sixteen, what does that mean?
Just coming to an age?
It means sixteen, still pure, still clean
Despite the current rage
Many things that tempt and try
Are facing you each day
Drugs, cheat, steal, lie
Some say that just the way
Daughter dear, you do what's right
You fill my heart with pride
Keep doing good with all you heart
Stay on the winning side
On this birthday let me say
I think that you're a queen
It's such a joy for me to say
My daughter's Sweet Sixteen

From Across the Street

Why is it we are sometimes too close to see?
I know my five daughters are beautiful
Many people have told me so
Why don't I more readily see the inner beauty of each?
I never miss the untidy room
I always notice the unmade bed
I see every time the clothes left on the floor
And the dishes left on the kitchen table
Of course, I compliment and praise them
I acknowledge their accomplishments
But why do some come overshadowed
By a complaint or criticism?
I saw them all together from across the street
There seemed to be so many
Five beautiful young girls
My heart began to pound and my eyes filled with tears
Suddenly the eternal potential of my daughters flooded over me
Five lovely, devoted and adoring wives and mothers
Five brilliant, diligent citizens of the world
Five women of great worth
They will know how to make beds

Where dirty clothes and dishes belong
And if I am blessed and lucky
And very very careful
They will know how to be
Those wonderful women I envisioned
Across the street

An Almost Perfect Life

What's up with my life?
It's not like those around me
It's different than most of my friends
It baffles and confounds me
I don't know what it was
I did or didn't do to deserve this
I think I'm just like everyone else
We all aim high but I rarely miss
Not hungry not homeless
No worries no strife
For now I'm just enjoying
An almost perfect life
What's up with my life?
Many around me suffer
So many troubles are part of each day
Am I lucky or just somehow tougher?
I don't understand why problems
Just seem to pass me by
My path so far is golden and straight
And I just don't understand why
Not helpless not hopeless no heartache no strife

For now I'm just enjoying An almost perfect life
No crying, no sighing, no pain, no rain
No tears, no fears, no sorrow
I'll face the challenges life has to give
With all the strength I can borrow- tomorrow
But right now I'll go on enjoying
The life that fate has sent me
I'll try to be strong if the good life is gone
And family and friends resent me
I'll recall this special, precious time
And no matter my trials and strife
I'll think I can climb back up again
To an almost perfect life

A Thanksgiving Prayer

As we sit at this table and feast with each other
Friends, sisters, brothers, father and mother
Our thoughts are turned to our Lord above
And we're thankful He gave us each other to love
We offer this prayer on this Thanksgiving Day
Let all our lives matter in every way
Let us be willing to feed Thy sheep
Let our feelings of love always run deep
Lord, let us thankful be, now and through eternity
For Thy love and tender caring
For the warmth of this home
And the meal we are sharing
We thank Thee for our strength and health
For our jobs and needed wealth
We thank Thee for our varied talents
For all our interests that give life balance
Let us remember our gifts from Thee
All that we have and hear and see
For all our blessings, great and small
Help us remember God gives us all
Let us be careful to not hurt a heart

Help us be faithful in doing our part
Help us remember we're each God's child
Let patience be long and tempers be mild
Let us go forth to serve Thee with might
Striving each day to do what is right
Let us humble our hearts in our searches
For strong testimonies, the truth of our churches
Now let us live life to its loftiest height
Always keeping Thy kingdom in sight
And knowing of all Thy gifts from above
The greatest and most important is love

Christmas

When I was young I used to wonder
How can Christmas get any better than this?
The shining tree with the presents under
And Santa Claus to fulfill every wish
When I was young the joy of the season
Was snowflakes and candy and goodies galore
I seldom stopped to think of the reason
We were having this holiday for
But as I grew up I understood Jesus
And worked very hard to give Him more thought
But with all the cooking and shopping and fuss
The Lord mattered less with each present I bought
I worried about money, how was I going to pay
For all of the joy I was buying today
But now that I'm older, I've started to know
That Christmas can't get any better than this

The spirit of Christ isn't tied with a bow
My family around me is true Christmas bliss
Yes, now that I'm old, I know so much more
The kiss of a grandchild is candy to me
Christ isn't found in a hot crowded store
It's people that matter to Him, don't you see
Nothing under the tree but in how much we love
Is our gift of thanks to our Savior above
He came to teach us, forgive us, redeem us
And his greatest wish
Is that we love and live life so we know
Only Heaven can be better than this

Free Agency

Free agency isn't free, everything has a price
Life is not a game of chance, a toss of a coin or roll of the dice
Everything we do, we're accountable for someday
Everything has a price and eventually we'll pay
Free agency isn't free, though it is a gift from God
It has some strings attached, although that may seem odd
Along with every blessing there is a law to keep
He gives us His commandments, we sow and then we reap
Free agency isn't free, our knowledge makes us pay
The Lord has always told us which laws we must obey
It's obedience to the laws that really sets us free
Will and strength to do what's right has always been the key
Free agency isn't free, decisions rule our life
One wrong choice can change a life of joy to one of strife
No one says life's easy, we do the best we can
Thank goodness with free agency, God gave a saving plan
Free agency's the way, we choose the good and right
When we choose repentance, we turn our light on bright
Free agency isn't free, for every act we pay
God's reward for righteous choices is joy that will stay and stay...

Don't You Know Me?

Don't you know me?
I've made mistakes it's true, but don't you know me?
All throughout my life, you've helped me get through strife
But do you know me?
Don't you know me?
Look past what seems to be and really know me
It brings me grief and tears that after all these years
You still don't know me
Don't you know me?
We've grown so ill at ease, seems you don't know me
The past is dead and gone, I'm trying to be strong
Don't you know me?
Try to know me
Our views won't always match, but seek to know me
I'm grown up, on my own, with values firm as stone
So please, just know me

Andrea's Shoes

Sent with a talent from God above
From the very beginning dance was your love
These dancing shoes worn completely out
Show what it was all about
Work, dedication, joy and strife
Many emotions were there in your life
All the coaches and partners you had
Some just wonderful, others quite bad
Taught you lessons in every way
That made you the woman you are today
Competition for you is done
But in some way you always won
There was knowledge to gain every day
And you were wise to see it that way
Your talents now you've passed on to others
You teach and train, you're a wife and a mother
Dance will always be in your heart
Part of your life from the end to the start
These dance shoes will help you always remember
Your dance life always a glowing ember
And you'll thank the Lord that your life was enhanced
By every move and step that you danced

Thoughts on Love and Relationships

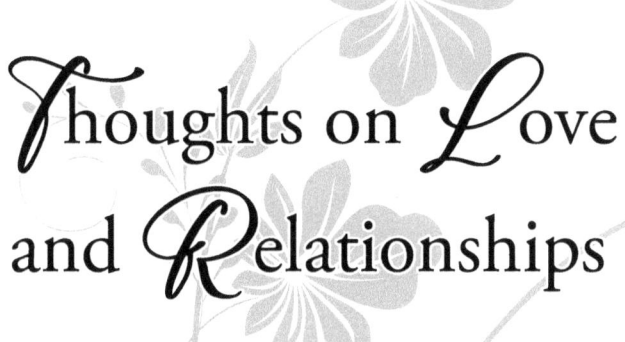

Are You the One?

Are you the one?
The one my teddy bear was forced to be
When he, my doll and I played family?
Are you the one?
The one I talked to in my mind all day
When "teen girl on a perfect date" I'd play?
Are You the One?
The one my mother prayed one day would find me?
The one she hoped would fill my life with glee
Are you the one?
The one my mind compared all others to
The one I think I somehow always knew
Are you the one?
The one who makes my feet not touch the ground
The one who makes my head spin, my heart pound
Are you the one?
The one I prayed so hard someday I'd find
The one who fits the model in my mind
Are you the one?
The one who fills my heart with warmth and light
The one who just might be my Mr. Right

Are you the one?
The one my future children might call Dad
The one who fits the dreams of love I've had
Are you the one?
You and I have only just begun
Our journey of discovery and fun
To see if I'm for you and you for me
If we are really meant to be
I can hardly wait to see
If you the one

Falling in Love

This falling in love, how does it happen?

A stranger becomes an acquaintance then the acquaintance becomes a friend. The friendship grows stronger and you find your mind wonders to her in idol moments. You find yourself smiling whenever she enters the room and you softly sigh when she leaves, hanging on to her image until the last possible moment. She brightens your days and disturbs your nights with thoughts of her, but what you trade for sleep is priceless. Without effort or will you have fallen in love. Expressions of that love comes in so many ways. Your arm around her waist, her small hand engulfed in the largeness of your own. A look from across the room when you're both busy. Your eyes meet and hold each other for a moment then release you to your tasks, but in that moment volumes have been silently spoken. A giggle, a hug. She presses her head against your heart and snuggles beneath your protective arm. You cradle her face in your hands as if it were a downy duckling. Her eyes down cast at first, slowly raise to meet your gaze and shine with approval of you and an impeding kiss. You bend down toward her, caressing her lips as gently as a butterfly brushes a rose. Your lips drink love from hers until you're sure every drop must be drained, but as your lips part you see in her eyes that she is more full of love after giving you all she had than she was a moment ago. Your love is the love that knows the joy of giving. The kind of love that knows giving the ultimate expression of love desires the giving of sacred vows in a sacred place. Only then is that gift of love the treasure God meant it to be. You know it is a privilege to feel that kind of love and to be entrusted to nurture it and care for it, to save it and protect it at any cost until the time is right for it to soar and fill the universe as yours will until it reaches heaven which is its home.

Lately You've Changed

I remember the look in your eye when I'd pass by
I remember the touch of your hand in mine
I remember you made my spirits fly
I remember that we always felt so fine
I remember the hours we spend on the phone
You told me you loved being with me
You asked me to be your very own
You told me our love was meant to be
I remember how I was the light of your life
I remember how loving me made your day
I remember we had very little strife
I remember we loved to laugh and play
But lately I miss that look in your eye
And lately at times we seem estranged
And lately I fear we'll say good bye
I remember, but lately you've changed
Looking closer, there are many lights in our life
Through the years our feelings have rearranged
As a family we know joy but also strife
We're in love so really what's changed
We're in love so nothing has changed

Come Fill Me With Your Love

Come fill me with your love –
look at me the way you did in our early years
Come fill me with your love –
speak to me with the tone that took away my fears
Come fill me with your love -
Say the things I took for granted then
But long for so much now
Come fill me with your love -
Treasure me the way you promised to
The day we made our vow
Protect me, take care of me,
convince me that your loving has no end
Be helper, be teacher, be sweetheart, be friend
Come fill me with your love -
For my cup which once was full is nearly dry
Come fill me with your love -
Nurture me and again the level will be high
Come fill me with your love -
And everything you need I will be to you
Come fill me with your love-
And I will fill you too and make our promise true

What is Love?

Sometimes love is a builder, like strong pillars that hold up a beautiful building or the cement that holds a dam together against great pressure keeping what is behind that wall of love safe and secure.

Sometimes love is a tidal wave, uncontrollably crushing everything in its path,

Uprooting and destroying the beach that existed before the wave began, ravaging the calm that should exist between sea and shore

Love can grow between two people but is it a good thing if several special relationships are sacrificed in its' name? Is love really that solitary? Is two all that matters? When walking down the path of love is it wise to burn bridges as we go, giving up what used to be so important? Love is a task, a balancing act enormously difficult. With much practice some can walk the path remaining calm water, strong pillars and keep on balance.

Love can build. Love can destroy.

Does Love Die?

How does love die, or does it? Maybe love needs to be exercised and worked to remain fit and strong. If that doesn't happen perhaps love just quietly slips off into a deep sleep with occasional dreams of by gone days when it was young, new, awake and alive. I suppose love can be awakened with a tender kiss like in fairy tales, but maybe that's only in stories. Perhaps love once asleep never awakens again but slumbers peacefully and gently on until without even noticing love has quietly and painlessly died.

A Crutch

I feel like a pair of crutches, created for just one thing.
There was a time when you didn't stand well without me.
I was always there, so necessary in your life
Here I am. Lean on me. I won't let you fall
Remember how glad you were to have me in that time of need?
You were so grateful. You loved me and maybe still do.
Now you say your legs are strong. You've cast me aside
seldom even thinking of the time you needed me so
much. You haven't even passed me on to someone else
who could use me. I guess that's the fate of crutches when
they have served their purpose, but lucky crutches
They don't have feelings

Friends

We're friends and that's as it should be
We can joke and laugh and talk
We're friends though we're a He and She
And a friendship's not something to knock
We're friends in a group and friends alone
We're friends and I'm glad that it's so
We're friends in person and friends on the phone
And our friendship will grow and grow
We're friends, I feel a bond with you
Though some would say that's not right
We're friends. I like to be with you
And that's something I'm not going to fight
We're friends and you can trust me
I'm not going to mess up your life
We're friends and I will never be
One to cause heartache and strife
So let's go on as we have been
There's no need to have any fears
Our relationship is special
We'll be friends throughout the years

Moderation

As I go through life meeting God's other children
I live my life in extremes
Black, white, high low
With only occasional in-betweens
Don't be that way you'll get hurt is the
constant warning that goes unheeded
My friends are truly that, not just acquaintances
My life is never flat but constantly dipping and climbing
The warnings are fair. I have been hurt.
Moderation in all things?
Love moderately, care moderately, live and even error moderately?
No, not for me!
Opposition in all things fits me better
So while some are enjoying moderately wonderful relationships
with their fellow beings in this life
I am soaring to heaven in many of my relationships
And I know it's heaven because I've also been to Hell

On the lighter side – For Fun

The Preacher

He steps to the pulpit and shouts Praise the Lord
   Repeating it often, who cares if we're bored
   He paces and stomps, waving arms wildly
   Doesn't he know that Jesus taught mildly?
His voice is monotonous, a dull Southern drawl
But the volume could make walls of Jericho fall
   Send him some money, he'll heal a deaf mute
But he heals best while wearing a handmade silk suit
He wants you to come to the front and be saved
Convinced by the things that he's ranted and raved
   Repent of your sins and come down to me
   If you're not here in person, touch your TV
   Keep sending in money from near and afar
 The work must go forth and he wants a new car
   Amazingly, Grace I've still yet to see
 A third world, blind leper healed live on TV

Snore

It's 3 o'clock in the mornin' and I'm lyin' here awake
If he don't stop his snorin' I'll hit him with a rake
Sure he has other minor faults, he drinks and stays out late
But his loud incessant snorin' is the one thing I can't take
Oh Lord, don't wanna hear that snore no more
It's not that I don't love him, I'm pretty sure I do
But if he don't stop that snorin' I don't know what I'll do
It's like a den of grizzlies is roaring in my bed
If he don't stop that snorin' he's gonna wake up dead
I think that I still love him, at least I hope I do
But when he starts that snorin', I wish for someone new
It was 3 o'clock in the mornin', I was naggin' him some more
He said "I can't help snorin'" and left and slammed the door
Now I wish I had that grizzly, could have him next to me
If he would just forgive me, how happy I would be
Oh Lord, I wanna hear that snore some more
So be nice to your snorer, keep him loved and close to home
If you're as mean as I was, Girl, you'll be alone
It's 3 o'clock in the mornin' and it's too still ta sleep
If I don't hear his snorin' I'm gunna start to weep
Sure, it was real annoyin', it always made me mad

But I'll take snorin' any day to feelin' this dang sad
Oh Lord, I wanna hear that snore some more
So be nice to your snorer, keep him loved and in your bed
Take it from his lonely gal who's cryin' awake instead
Please Lord, let me hear that snore some more
Can't live without that snore no more

The Hulkling

She looked like a duckling. Her black inch and a half long hair stood straight up like the fuzzy down you see on baby ducks on the Discovery Channel. She had the kind of blue eyes you know will stay blue not the smokey blue that usually turn brown. In truth, she was the fifth absolutely darling daughter to arrive at the Hale home where her parents were recognized experts at producing beautiful little girls. Everyone thought so, especially their several grandparents.

They named her Andrea and for about eighteen months she was a total delight.

She slept like...well, like a baby, ate like there was no tomorrow, had the disposition of a miniature saint and was growing into a textbook perfect toddler.

No one knows why the change took place. It was gradual yet seemed rapid. The Darling Duckling became the Incredible Hulk. Not in size but in behavior. One minute she'd be happy, contentedly playing with her doll and blanket and the next she would be wildly throwing the doll on the floor in a fit of rage. Blocks were kicked across the room and books torn apart.

Besides changing moods like the Hulk, we wondered if she didn't also possess his strength as well. Little knuckles would appear over the counter top, then a head full of dark brown hair followed by two sky blue eyes then the cute little nose and darling grin. Having done a chin up on the kitchen counter that would make an Army Drill Sergeant proud, this amazingly strong little girl could hold herself suspended, feet off the floor, for several minutes. When she would decide a sisters' toy should be hers, there was no getting it out of her iron grip. A grip that sometimes closed around the soft cheek of an older sister or neighborhood child's face, often bringing blood and serious complaints.

She wasn't always the Hulk though. Often she was a household terrorist pulling of such capers as sopping all the water out of the toilet with her clothes or those of a furious sister. The clever plan of turning her dresser toward the wall so she couldn't get to the clothes backfired when her strength allowed her to simply tip it over. One day during a seemingly innocent nap she tore her mattress to shreds.

Attempts at discipline rarely produced the desired change. If she was confined to her room, the curtains, hardware and all were yanked from the wall or the door was chipped and dented by kicks or blows from whatever was handy. Her most annoying and fairly common trick was to take off her messy diaper and deposit its contents all over the room. There always seemed to be enough for the floor, walls and bed and some left over to put down the heat vent so when her highly frustrated mother had spent hours and a fortune on cleaning supplies to counter the attack, there was an odor mysteriously lingering in the air when the furnace clicked on.

The Siege continued on. Though the list of offenses seemed endless, the "Hulk" was not. Happily, through love, patience and yes, some professional help, along with a miracle time-out stool that for some unbelievable and unknown reason she would not get off, the Hulk was slowly replaced by a bright blue eyed, highly intelligent little sweetheart. By the time she was five she was so improved that her mother hated to see her go off to school because she would be without her little "bestie friend."

At the first parent teacher conference of kindergarten her parents were almost afraid to ask if Andrea had any friends or if she had made anyone bleed. They doubted the teacher really knew who they were talking about. "Andrea, little blonde…" they started to explain. The teachers said, "of course we know Andrea. Darling, smart girl, tons of friends, behaves so well." Who? What? She still has an occasional outburst, or snit, as they came to be called. Don't we all? But now at eleven she is a beautiful young girl who dances like a pro, gets excellent grades, takes responsibility for her room and cooks like a little Julia Child. Her bright blue eyes sparkle as she laughs, as we all can now, about her early escapades. She is full of love and personality and keeps life interesting, so maybe crossing the Incredible Hulk with a Fuzzy Duckling makes a great kid after all.

www.ingramcontent.com/pod-product-compliance
Lightning Source LLC
LaVergne TN
LVHW041559070526
838199LV00046B/2051